LOVE ALONE

18 Elegies For Rog

Paul Monette and Roger Horwitz
Monte Oliveto
Autumn 1983

LOVE
ALONE

18 ELEGIES FOR ROG

by Paul Monette

ST. MARTIN'S PRESS
NEW YORK

"No Goodbyes" first appeared in *Bay Windows*.
"The Worrying" and "The Very Same" first appeared in *American Poetry Review*.

EDNA ST. VINCENT MILLAY, *Collected Poems*, Harper & Row, 1956, from "Fatal Interview," XXX, lines 5–8.
DYLAN THOMAS, *Collected Poems*, New Directions, 1971, from "Do Not Go Gentle Into That Good Night," line 14.
WILLIAM CARLOS WILLIAMS, *The Collected Earlier Poems*, New Directions, 1951, from "Tract," lines 69–70.
D. H. LAWRENCE, "New Mexico," reprinted in *D. H. Lawrence and New Mexico*, Peregrine Smith, 1982, page 96.
RAINER MARIA RILKE, *Duino Elegies*, translated by C. F. McIntyre, University of California, 1968, from *Elegy VIII*, lines 64–69.
C. P. CAVAFY, *The Complete Poems*, Harcourt, Brace, 1961, translated by Rae Dalven, from "For Ammonis, Who Died at 29 in 610," lines 13–16.
ROBINSON JEFFERS, *The Selected Letters 1897–1962*, Johns Hopkins, 1968, from a letter to Frederick M. and Maud Clapp, October 1950, page 327.
PINDAR, "Pythian Ode VIII," from *The Greek World* by Eliot Porter and Peter Levi, Aurum Press, 1981.
GERARD MANLEY HOPKINS, *The Poems*, Oxford, 1970, from "Thou Art Indeed Just, Lord," line 14.

Design by Claire B. Counihan

LIBRARY OF CONGRESS
Library of Congress Cataloging-in-Publication Data

Monette, Paul.
    Love alone : 18 elegies for Rog / by Paul Monette.
        p. cm.
    ISBN 0-312-01472-4 : $14.95
    1. Elegiac poetry, American.   2. Love poetry, American.
    3. Homosexuality, Male—Poetry.   4. AIDS (Disease)—Patients-
Poetry.   I. Title.
PS3563.0523L65 1988
811'.54—dc19   87-27517
                                                                      CIP

First Edition
10 9 8 7 6 5 4 3 2 1

Love can not fill the thickened lung with breath,
Nor clean the blood, nor set the fractured bone;
Yet many a man is making friends with death
Even as I speak, for lack of love alone.

—EDNA ST. VINCENT MILLAY

CONTENTS

PREFACE

Above all I am not concerned with poetry.
My subject is War, and the pity of War.
The poetry is in the pity.
                    —WILFRED OWEN, *1918*

Wilfred Owen's *Preface* to the poems he wrote in 1917 and 1918 is the best caution I know against beauty and eloquence. He begs us not to read his anthem for the doomed youth of his generation as a decorous celebration of heroes. Decorum is the contemptible pose of the politicians and preachers, the hypocrite slime whose grinning hatred slicks this dying land like rotten morning dew. I do not presume on the nightmare of Owen's war—may the boys of Flanders be spared all comparison—and I don't pretend to have written the anthem of my people. But I would rather have this volume filed under AIDS than under Poetry, because if these words speak to anyone they are for those who are mad with loss, to let them know they are not alone.

Roger Horwitz, my beloved friend, died on 22 October 1986, after nineteen months of fighting the ravages of AIDS. He was forty-four years old, the happiest man I ever knew. He fought with an immensity of spirit that transfigured us who loved him. On his grave are Plato's last words on Socrates: *the wisest and justest and best.* Rog had a constitutional aversion to bullshit and was incapable of being unkind. Though he held two degrees from Harvard—a Ph.D. in Comparative Literature and a law degree—he made no show of it. The only thing he ever bragged about were his three bohemian years in Paris in his early twenties, and he didn't so much boast of them as endlessly give them away.

These elegies were written during the five months after he died, one right after the other, with hardly a half day's pause between. Writing them quite literally kept me alive, for the only time I wasn't wailing and trembling was when I was hammering at these poems. I have let them stand as raw as they came. But because several friends have wished for a few commas or a stanza break here and there, I feel I should make a comment on their form. I don't mean them to be impregnable, though I admit I want them to allow no escape, like a hospital room, or indeed a mortal illness.

In the summer of 1984 Roger and I were in Greece together, and for both of us it was a peak experience that left us dazed and slightly giddy. We'd been together for ten years, and life was very sweet. On the high bluff of ancient Thera, looking out across the southern Aegean toward Africa, my hand grazed a white marble block covered edge to edge with Greek characters, line after precise line. The marble was tilted face up to the weather, its message slowly eroding in the rain. "I hope somebody's recorded all this," I said, realizing with a dull thrill of helplessness that this *was* the record, right here on this stone.

When I began to write about AIDS during Roger's illness, I wanted a form that would move with breathless speed, so I could scream if I wanted and rattle on and empty my Uzi into the air. The marbles of Greece kept coming back to mind. By the time Roger died the form was set—not quite marble, not quite Greek—but it was in my head that if only a fragment remained in the future, to fade in the sulfurous rain, it would say how much I loved him and how terrible was the calamity.

The story that endlessly eludes the decorum of the press is the death of a generation of gay men. What is written here is only one man's passing and one man's cry, a warrior burying a warrior. May it fuel the fire of those on the front lines who mean to prevail, and of their friends who stand in the fire with them. We will not be bowed down or erased by this. I learned too well what it means to be a people, learned in the joy of my best friend what all the meaningless pain and horror cannot take away—that all there is is love. Pity us not.

Los Angeles
29 June 1987

I

HERE

everything extraneous has burned away
this is how burning feels in the fall
of the final year not like leaves in a blue
October but as if the skin were a paper lantern
full of trapped moths beating their fired wings
and yet I can lie on this hill just above you
a foot beside where I will lie myself
soon soon and for all the wrack and blubber
feel still how we were warriors when the
merest morning sun in the garden was a
kingdom after Room 1010 war is not all
death it turns out war is what little
thing you hold on to refugeed and far from home
oh sweetie will you please forgive me this
that every time I opened a box of anything
Glad Bags One-A-Days KINGSIZE was
the worst I'd think will you still be here
when the box is empty Rog Rog who will
play boy with me now that I bucket with tears
through it all when I'd cling beside you sobbing
you'd shrug it off with the quietest *I'm still
here* I have your watch in the top drawer
which I don't dare wear yet help me please
the boxes grocery home day after day
the junk that keeps men spotless but it doesn't
matter now how long they last or I
the day has taken you with it and all
there is now is burning dark the only green
is up by the grave and this little thing
of telling the hill I'm here oh I'm here

NO GOODBYES

for hours at the end I kissed your temple stroked
your hair and sniffed it it smelled so clean we'd
washed it Saturday night when the fever broke
as if there was always the perfect thing to do
to be alive for years I'd breathe your hair
when I came to bed late it was such pure you
why I nuzzle your brush every morning because
you're in there just like the dog the night
we unpacked the hospital bag and he skipped
and whimpered when Dad put on the red
sweater *Cover my bald spot will you*
you'd say and tilt your head like a parrot
so I could fix you up always always
till this one night when I was reduced to
I love you little friend here I am my
sweetest pea over and over spending all our
endearments like stray coins at a border
but wouldn't cry then no choked it because
they all said hearing was the last to go
the ear is like a wolf's till the very end
straining to hear a whole forest and I
wanted you loping off whatever you could
still dream to the sound of me at 3 P.M.
you were stable still our favorite word
at 4 you took the turn WAIT WAIT I AM
THE SENTRY HERE nothing passes as long as
I'm where I am we go on death is
a lonely hole two can leap it or else
or else there is nothing this man is mine
he's an ancient Greek like me I do
all the negotiating while he does battle
we are war and peace in a single bed
we wear the same size shirt it can't it can't
be yet not this just let me brush his hair

it's only Tuesday there's chicken in the fridge
from Sunday night he ate he slept oh why
don't all these kisses rouse you I won't won't
say it all I will say is goodnight patting
a few last strands in place you're covered now
my darling one last graze in the meadow
of you and please let your final dream be
a man not quite your size losing the whole
world but still here combing combing
singing your secret names till the night's gone

YOUR SIGHTLESS DAYS

Blind eyes could blaze like meteors and be gay
—DYLAN THOMAS

I remember clearly deciding not to see
anymore myself this out of sheer protest
or only see what I could tell you the whole of
art was out so was anything new the buff
hillside gone to grass was just our speed
but of course I was always minimizing
as if to say there's nothing to see today
it's the same old thing Rog sycamore's bare
park full of Seurats but hey feel that breeze
and knowing how clear Aegean blue your eyes were
please I know what I watched go out but even
when it struck us down blacked our windows
like an air raid even then your glimmering half
sight was so seductive *What do you see*
I'd ask you coaxing every street sign like
they were glyphs off a ruined temple night
would fall you'd frown *Are the lights on Paul*
and tear my heart all the Bette Davis lines
out to get us but oh my dearest every one
was on spots flashes searches long white tubes
like the swords in *Star Wars* candlepower fit
for a Byzantine saint and still so dim the dark
so jealous of life and then out of nowhere
a neon day of LA sun we're out strolling
you stop peer impish intent as a hawk
and say *I see you* just like that and THEN
I toss my blinders and drink the world like water
till the next dark up and down for half a year
the left one gone in April overnight
two millimeters on the right side saved
and we fought for those that knife of light

6

and beaten ground raging for day like the
Warsaw ghetto all summer long I dripped
your veins at 4 and midnight watching every
drop as if it was sight itself so did we
win did we lose you died with the barest
shadows oh I know but even then we hoped
a cataract laser might give us a glint
would not see night as the way of the world
and what have I seen since your blindness my
love just that my love requires no eyes so
why am I tapping this thin white cane of outrage
through crowds of sighted fools the pointless trees
and the awful dusk unlifting some few colors
bright as razor blades trying to make me look
I'm shut tight Oedipus-old leave me alone
I have somehow gotten it all wrong because
when you were the blackest blind you laughed *laughed*
groped your way and stared the noon sun down
How are you jerks would ask *Read Job* you'd say
a gleam in every good hour pulling out puns
and Benny jokes and fighting to read the charts
knowing the worst had fallen you'd hoot on the phone
and wrestle the dog so the summer was still
the summer Rog see how you saw us through

GARDENIAS

pain is not a flower pain is a root
and its work is underground where the moldering
proceeds the bones of all our joy winded
and rained and nothing grows a whole life's love
that longed to be an orchard forced to lie
like an onion secret sour in the mine of pain
the ore veined out there's just these tunnels shot
with roots but then we were never gardeners
were we planters waterers cleanup crew
more yard boys three bucks an hour than rose queens
still the place was the vale of Arcady to us
and after all a man can plant a stone here
and it'll sprout but gardenias now those vellum
Billie Holiday prom flowers what a shock
to learn they grew on *trees* well bushes then
we urned one in the shade of the Chinese elm
watered and watered the white blooms wafting May
to mid-August now and then you'd bring one in
floating in a bowl and leave it on my desk
by such small tokens did the world grow green
and the Billie Holiday song is this I'm jealous
of all the time I didn't know you yet
and the month since so full of risible scalding
blankness I crave it more that secondhand past
oh you can keep the lovers the far countries
but you young you twenty you in Paris
with a poem in your boot if I could have that
really be there then beside you or waving
across Boulevard Saint-Germain I'd face these
dead days longer the cave of all that's left
enough now as to gardenias look this is
such a cliché but one happened to break
in October by then I was bringing them in
leaving them at your bedside between the Kleenex

and the talking clock *Smell it good now Rog*
it's the last one fourth day yellow and smutty
yet I gave you one last whiff right under
your nose while you talked to Jaimee then
you died a week later and that next day
I was out in the garden to die of the pain
but wait what is this Thomas Hardy a furled
gardenia just coming out which I bowled by
the bed I sleep now just where you slept curled
in the selfsame spot and that one lasted through
the funeral next week a third billowed out
what is this *Twilight Zone* which I laid on
the grave as if I was your date for the prom
which I would've been if we'd ever been 18
but for all the spunk of the three gardenias
still the pain is not a flower and digs like
a spade in stony soil no earthly reason
not a thing will come of it but a slag heap
and a pit and the deepest root the stuff of witch
banes winds and winds its tendril about my heart
I promise you all the last gardenias Rog
but they can't go on like this they've stopped they know
the only garden we'll ever be is us and it's
all winter they tried they tried but oh the ice
of my empty arms my poor potato dreams

THE WORRYING

ate me alive day and night these land mines
all over like the toy bombs dropped on the
Afghans little Bozo jack-in-the-boxes
that blow your hands off 3 A.M. I'd go
around the house with a rag of ammonia
wiping wiping crazed as a housewife on *Let's*
Make a Deal the deal being PLEASE DON'T MAKE
HIM SICK AGAIN faucets doorknobs the phone
every lethal thing a person grips and leaves
his prints on scrubbed my hands till my fingers
cracked washed apples ten times ten no salad but
iceberg and shuck the outer two thirds someone
we knew was brain dead from sushi so stick
to meatloaf creamed corn spuds whatever we
could cook to death DO NOT USE THE D WORD
EVEN IN JEST when you started craving deli
I heaved a sigh because salami was so de-
germed with its lovely nitrites to hell with
cholesterol that's for people way way over
the hill or up the hill not us in the vale
of borrowed time yet I was so far more gone
than you nuts in fact ruinous as a supermom
with a kid in a bubble who can't play and ten
years later can't work can't kiss can't laugh
but his room's still clean every cough every
bump would nothing ever be nothing again
cramming you with zinc and Häagen-Dazs so wild
to fatten you up I couldn't keep track of
what was medicine what old wives' but see
THERE WAS NO MEDICINE only me and to
circle the wagons and island the last of our
magic spoon by spoon nap by nap till we
healed you as April heals drinking the sun
I was Prospero of the spell of day-by-day

and all of this just the house worry peanuts
to what's out there and you with the dagger at
your jugular struggling back to work jotting
your calendar two months ahead penciling
clients husbanding husbanding inching back
and me agape with the day's demises who
was swollen who gone mad ringing you on
the hour how are you compared to ten noon
one come home and have blintzes petrified
you'd step in an elevator with some hacking
CPA the whole world ought to be masked
please I can't even speak of the hospital fear
fists bone white the first day of an assault
huddled by your bed like an old crone empty-
eyed in a Greek square black on black the waiting
for tests the chamber of horrors in my head
my rags and vitamins dumb as leeches how did
the meningitis get in where did I slip up
what didn't I scour I'd have swathed the city
in gauze to cushion you no man who hasn't
watched his cruelest worry come true in a room
with no door can ever know what doesn't
die because they lie who say it's over
Rog it hasn't stopped at all are you okay
does it hurt what can I do still still I
think if I worry enough I'll keep you near
the night before Thanksgiving I had this
panic to buy the plot on either side of us
so we won't be cramped that yard of extra grass
would let us breathe THIS IS CRAZY RIGHT but
Thanksgiving morning I went the grave two over
beside you was six feet deep ready for the next
murdered dream so see the threat was real
why not worry worry is like prayer is like
God if you have none they all forget there's
the other side too twelve years and not once

to fret WHO WILL EVER LOVE ME that was
the heaven at the back of time but we had it
here now black on black I wander frantic
never done with worrying but it's mine it's
a cure that's not in the books are you easy
my stolen pal what do you need is it
sleep like sleep you want a pillow a cool
drink oh my one safe place there must be
something just say what it is and it's yours

READINESS

Go now
I think you are ready
—William Carlos Williams

pre-need they call it at Forest Lawn pre-dead
is what they mean but they aren't all poodled
like Liberace a bit overripe but truly
convinced they're the launching pad hands slick
with Jergen's beaming all-God's-children
my pre-need meeting's next Wednesday with Bill
who hopes on the phone you're in a better world
and wants the gay market we'll go with the Old
North Church not *that* one they have their own
coffin polished steel closed no viewing no
embalming want to rot with my blood inside
means I can't be dressed but naked is quite
proper I'm not going out for dinner bare
is how I sleep nudist I wander the house
lap the pool check what's left in the mirror
3 concrete linings to pick from CA law
no sinking allowed 2 are tight as nuclear
shelters watersealed the third slatted on top
so the earth fills in yes yes more earth and
junk steel for the casket one wants to get back
to the soil quick for that is where we meet
no flowers well a spray of gardenias perhaps
but the floral part rankles especially after
I hated the flower garbage on your grave
besides we're out of the hothouse biz
earth wind water is all we are now I learned
this lingo for you Rog time-of-need alas
stripped Episcopal will do for the post-mortem
very stripped a little ashes-to-ashes no
I AM THE LIFE He's not no hymns no organ

just poems will's all signed with Dickensian
cut-outs medical power of attorney in case
of dementia every day I think of a new
way to get ready I'm ready as a fucking
fire department toss in please a pebble
from Delphi and a hunk of Brighton Rock
just like my friend plot's all paid for deed
the whole bit not a piece of real estate
expected to boom or condo-ize new address
Revelation thirty-two-seventy-five Space 1
2's you with 4 bristling evergreens at the
compass points to guard us therefore 1 P.M.
for the ceremony so the shadows dapple like
they did for you with the Valley bathed in light
epitaph name no middle initial date then
FOR 12 YEARS ALL THE LOVE IN THE WORLD WAS HI
OTHERWISE HE WAS A WRITER HERE I AM ROG
not Yeats exactly but there won't be horsemen
passing only if we're lucky some far-off
men of our sort generations hence a pair
of dreamy types strolling among the hill graves
for curiosity's sake this well may be
in a time when dying is not all day and every
house riven and they'll laugh *Here's 2 like us*
won't that be lovely Rog make the grass shiver
like the dog's coat oh yes the dog goes to
my brother hoping the leash law's unenforced
pills I still have to get pills for the ten
contingencies of lingering hemlock
would be choice for Platonic reasons but
a cocked .32 will do in a pinch does this all
sound like I'm checking out oh darling no
I'm not half ready to leave us here without
us all told but the sickness is near sometimes
as the wall of this room things have to be done
I used my optimism up keeping you alive

14

all but this no matter what else we lie
together believing less than nothing now
I haven't the ghost of a lease on a better
world though I cry out your name and beg for
signs I am only prepared for wind and water
I put my house in order inch by inch
if it comes when it comes I'll be on the
diving board toes over the edge my gleaming
broken body all the details done with
one last dazzled thought of you in the sun
be wind and rain with me ready for deepest
darkness no matter how nothing not alone

HALF LIFE

exactly half the phenomenal world is gone
look you can see it take anything *anything*
roses a half corona of petals red lush
half black rot now the aching mountains Heidi
on the east slope west face strip-mined singed
as if by lava houses up and down the street
half pink stucco curtains breezing the windows
half smithereens dead toys melted lawn chairs
in my case I think it's the left side closest
to you in bed I get up and half of me doesn't
work I drag me like a broken wing my good
eye sees flesh and green the dead eye an X-
ray gaping at skeletons I could bear it
if the fugue went back and forth but the skull's
the bedrock truth just as I'm the friendless
kid who never made it out of Andover MA
and all the while you are getting more whole Rog
even as the world is cleaved in two I open
the door to the morning and half the city's
Capri and half Buchenwald how is it you
so vanished so cut down such proof of the end
of all gentle men how is it you spring full-blown
from a thousand fragments it's like picking up
a shard of red-black vase off a Greek hillside
looks like part of a sandal and a girl's long hair
in a flash the white-stone city rises entire
around you full of just men who live to be
90 the buried pieces fit I blow up pictures
to 5 by 7 and stare in your eyes and you're
all there more finely boned more grown than I
and always looking at me the cavorting dunce
of the Nikon wild as a tourist with ten minutes
left in Rome life's mostly snapshots oh how
I want the rest of me to be the rest of you

but cut in half like this how can I I read
your '80 diary its limpid accounts the blessed
dailiness gold as winter sunset and you say
Paul had a bad meeting or *Paul's upset*
about NOTHING I SWEAR IT WAS NOTHING AT ALL
I was totally intact and didn't know and
now the sun's cold as the moon and rivers
die mid-cataract the species from N to
Z are extinct not a tiger left leafing
two months through '80 clucking at your mood
swings I practically forget it's like you're
going to walk in and compass the world again
and the west face of everything will torrent
with orchids and streams of honey a Bengal
roaring from the escarpment Rog I am not
reconciled not a millimeter unless
you count the dead-fish fin that was my hand
the stump of my running foot this side
of me that's halfway there see I must've loved
life too much in our time doubtless this is
to balance me out so I live in what's left of
the evidence not out there in the rotting
garden the firebombed street and Plato's myth
of lovers the fated meeting of equal halves
is a tale for lonely kids there's no act III
the sundering with its howl that never ends
waits till the pictures are shot to sever east
and west like a man bound spreadeagle to four
horses bolting for the corners of an earth
half ash half mad nothing what it was mine
the skull in the field and once I had it all

BLACK XMAS

Scrooge bolts upright from the dream runs to the ice-
skinned casement flings it wide and bellows at
a boy below WHAT DAY IS IT *Why Christmas
sir of course* and the miser gasps stares up
the snowdust street the bells are pealing and
he chokes out *There's still time* and goes about
his delirious redeeming no shortages
when there's still time a toyshop hums on every
corner flocks of geese in the poulterer's blood-
yard the lame are hoisted on their fathers
shoulders and have their pick of the fattest we
had three like that '83 César with his first
scatterburst of lesions '84 prone on
the sofa with his leg blimped twice its size
how we showered him with Armani shirts
and leather like beaten cream by next November
he was gone and '85 was yours Rog still
still time home after 2 months in and the gift
not anywhere near the tree but the newest drug
rarer than myrrh drunk out of I.V. bottles
6 times a day because they hadn't got a
pill yet the elixir that would give us 10
months more Cambridge the first Xmas my true
love gave to me a parakeet in a wire cage
swinging from a pine branch beside a tin angel
the holiday wasn't your cup of tea I know
not a shopper hopeless at wrapping living
as spare as Thoreau yet you gave me a bird
and a flute of Brighton Rock the furthest things
from Saks in all the world and otherwise
indulged my breathless mid-December binge
open house the 24th presents by the
boxcar again and again I'd tell you it's
not about baby Jesus Rog you have to

take the X out of Xmas and not just to
counter a Jew's rolled eyes no Scrooge's merry
nephew is truer than Luke *The only day
Uncle when all men seem to know they're fellow-
passengers* and we were so boundless you and I
it had to spill over once a year ashimmer
with bathos turkey and mince stocking for Puck
Mormon choir in the background and those guys
for chrissakes want us dead but now ah well
there is no more time and the third ghost with
his bony finger reading the tomb like Braille
is the dream from which we shall not wake this
year because I burned a blue candle eight days
running red and green have exited the spectrum
this is not to say Tiny Tim will never walk
upright or that skinflints colonels and Mormons
can't in the nick of time open the upper
floors of their pitiful mansions house the drifted
feed the lost be for a night innkeepers
but we are past redeeming long since twined
our presents each to each the hair cut to pay
for a watch fob watch hocked for a bone comb
giving over trading off emptying out
our daily fare for 20 months to learn how
little a man can get by on no one day
will do it love costs years the rest of it all
is Toys-Я-Us chill buffets for grazing
blue-flocked trees in empty lots so little
time to bear the heart so vast the desert

THE VERY SAME

the wrongest of the wrong things said that day
as I stepped from the chapel an idiot cousin
once-removed jiggled my shoulder *time to turn
the page* intoned like it's all been so appalling
we must hasten now to the land of brunch
there to recover our BMWs our zest for
winning and half-acre closets sorry I'm
booked weeks later still fuming with retorts
BUT THIS *IS* MY PAGE IT CANNOT BE TURNED
then start hearing similar from other bimbos
gotta turn the page Paul is this shit from
the Bible the sayings of Dr. Kübler-Ross
has Donohue done a show on it maybe
a ring of widows all walks of life neatly
combining real estate aerobics and young
blue-collar bowling dates spare me the pop
coping skills this page is all that's left of time
there *was* no page before I caught you the book
was nothing but cover painfully thin and
hopelessly derivative there's something French
in all of this perhaps *la vie continue*
well no it doesn't not if you freeze it in its
tracks think of this turnless page like Audubon's
elephant folio where the eagle is life-size
or a gilded Burgundian leaf of hours painted
with a one-hair brush for the whole last half
of the 1400s and no bigger than a 3 × 5
dear friend I didn't become your blood-brother
lightly mine ticks just like yours but a beat
slower the geiger of Death crackles in every
room yet He cannot seem to tell who's who
as you used to say in your cranked-up bed
playful astonished *But we're the same person
when did that happen* with Death's signals jammed

I and my page have eluded the dart awhile
Russians in bughouses write their poems on soap
with burnt matches then get them by heart then
wash in muddy water think what they would do
with a whole page no room left on ours edge
to edge with our growing interchangeability
what you would do I think is make a paper
glider go to the brink of a high green place
let it cavort the updrafts lulling itself
by lightness to the valley floor below
while I am more likely to paper the walls
with mine scrawling *why* and *where are you*
in our common blood how shall we compromise
would a kite do do you think riding its string
in the upper air and don't forget there's
an eagle on it and the monk's gilt borders
my blood-cries are too high up to read now
oh what a page Rog how can they not see
I am only still here to be with you
my best my only page scribbled on cirrus
the high air soaring in its every word

NEW YEAR'S AT LAWRENCE'S GRAVE

*What splendour! Only the tawny eagle
could really sail out into the splendour of it
all.*

—D. H. LAWRENCE

FOR BETTY SENESCU

Santa Fe was awful but don't go by me
I was just trying to get *here* the turquoise
boutique rug hunger gave me the bends fast
the strut of the Malibu skiers the bleach desert
not north enough not high enough I wanted
my nose to bleed the powder dry of blue snow
to frost and crack my hands up State 68
rippling beside the Rio Grande scarce wide
enough for a proper river no melt yet
so why the rush thus tamely you rise up to
the Taos plain the shock so sudden you jettison
your booster stage without even thinking WAIT
aloft in pure space and the higher you climb
toward Lawrence the savage alluvial moon
of Jupiter on your left stretches to Arizona
the sacred mountains wall the east piñon-crowded
snow-slashed older than we can dream now take
the last dirt track to Kiowa eagle land
for sure rutting to Frieda's ranch bought for
a song specific the autograph MS of *Sons
and Lovers* fair-traded to Mrs. Dodge
three rude cabins on a piney knoll pasture
below where Susan the cow switched flies all
plain as a clod of earth the drop-jaw view
millennial remorseless if that is your
sort of beauty then here is where to come
preferably with a spot on the lung and Pan's
pipe for a pen the final climb on foot

switchbacks the white hill the chapel up top
snug as a woodshed *chapel*'s wrong *shrine* oh
please *place* is all you need but not as in
final resting nothing could be further
off a stucco eagle caps the roofpeak
unless it's a phoenix the window in the eave's
the pinwheel hub of a tractor tire unglazed
inside was yellow once faded as Assisi
the altar cask silver-paint with DHL
incised a half-inch deep just above in a
shallow niche a second eagle neck cracked
east window a daisy-streaked wagon wheel
lowly offerings everywhere pine cones rock
chips acorns a single long-dead rose like the
windfall of tempests a glacier's lavish spoor
from us Rog I left the first day a double
sprig of evergreen next morning two downed
oak leaves parchment brown and flawless gathered
them off the hill like a deer and prayed open-eyed
Lorenzo teach me fire let me go out
burning he was your age Rog sang himself
to sleep like a canary in a coal mine
and the twist of fate versus him and Frieda
and you and me is the writer got left behind
in our casc also not such a grcat canary
in blue snowlight at this year's close I sobbed
and sobbed for us all the New Year's deadborn
way up here the date that counts is the one
that follows the hyphen as our one sere day
is 10/22 Lorenzo went in April
five months shy of forty-five and you
just thirty days I'm so rapacious of time
I hoard the extra four months as if they
weren't like everything else blown away in
the first good wind I wander graveyards now
like a math quiz figuring who we've beaten

23

I came to Lawrence for having about the same
to prove a man can leave the world burned clean
at forty-four and then the long climb down
the sun's rim the bare lace branches of the
cottonwoods like a line of Indian dancers
at the brink of every stream the horses in ones
and twos in meadows so wide you can see
the curve of the planet all the vastness Lawrence
never got enough of why is it given
to me whose soul is smashed to bits such doused
and dwindled fire a man who could write about
anything and the god in it would seethe
and drool with lust where is the phoenix now
now is the day of his rising or we are
all dead driving back to Taos I hung
a right and crossed the moon to the gorge bridge
maybe thirty miles upriver from the last
look remember how un-Grande it seemed well
here it was a river of flame in a rift
in Jupiter seven hundred feet below
a ribbon of jade and whitecap everything takes
forever and not one man with a spare minute
so bereft is the old year Rog your bullet
in its heart *Perhaps if I came back to New*
Mexico I would get up again says Lawrence
dying in Vence and see how he came back
just ashes years are born without him still
years don't care how rifted time has grown they
thrive on ashes pity this tremendous sky
this thundering country its goat-god is gone
long may its endless distance gray and ochre
ease his native spirit if only you
were here Rog it's the sort of beauty we
always walked in arm in arm we'd read him
out loud and bring him back I can't alone

the ashes of too much grief have choked the song
of mountains in me there are men who still
belong here oh eagle-flame of Taos
why have you wasted your splendor on me

II

THREE RINGS

*Who has twisted us like this, so that—
no matter what we do—we have the bearing
of a man going away? As on the last hill
that shows him all his valley for the last time,
he turns, stands still and lingers, so we live,
forever saying farewell.*
                                    —RAINER MARIA RILKE

before I left you I slipped off the ring
the nurse had taped to your finger so it
wouldn't get lost the last day you think I'd
forget I forget nothing was there the day
Dad gave it to you Chestnut St a continent
ago there when you said in the bathtub ten
years later sobbed really *If something happens
to me I guess this should go to* your brother
then your nephew still our best hope with his
sister of a future that will call us back
unencumbered just for love something was
already happening of course tearing rents
in the sky riddling the diamond-beveled
sea with flaws till the art of voyaging
was lost roads out of any town grew thick
with weeds one was stuck where one had got to
only so far and no further this was the
rule some people were left in train stations
with nothing in all directions but kangaroos
some in howdahs some in rickshaws sorry
folks end of the line the stone was a sapphire
won in a horse race I handed it over
on a bright clear morning my duty done
it didn't destroy me like several thousand
other things the lawyer's cards the magnifier
perhaps because my own fingers were bare
as birchbark then a week later I NEED A

MOURNING RING longing you see for an age of
widows in veils thick as bedsheets but where
do you go if you're not the sort who rings up
Tiffany's every time a saucer breaks day
by day I saw it clearer two thin bands
of gold with onyx between ah who has time
to shop in the murderous round of going noplace
then I went to Taos everything seemed to be
turquoise at first amber stalactite green
at last I found a Zuni jet-and-silver
barely fit my pinkie just ten bucks I
wasn't all that high-minded couldn't keep
one long enough my high school zircon vanished
before I hit Yale you'd have to follow me
with a metal-sweeper to keep me ringed
and buckled then the last day the last shop
and there it was the very thing black jade
banded in gold three fifty good god no
I'll lose it on the plane besides it's just
for the picturesque like keeping a stuffed cat
on the hearth getting more and more eccentric
till you gather the mail in your underpants
and stare white-eyed at passing trucks don't buy
things to be buried with anyway who can
you trust in the travertine cellars where men
go to sleep in eggwhite satin who counts
fingers after the lid's shut all the same
if fit me perfect and what's a Visa for
if not to go a little mad think of
the cabfare one is saving staying home
for the rest of time so the Zuni went into
my pocket I flexed the jade hand clever
as a showgirl baubled by a sheik of course
I knew right along it wouldn't touch the pain
it was just a game but one hungers so
for ritual that's portable you can't walk out

with tapers burning not to the 7-Eleven you want
to be brazen and secret all at once like a ring
back in LA I decided to keep a perfect
circle and bury the jet in the grass above
your folded arms so many along the way
had fashioned shanties living their level best
chained to a ring in the pavement begging with
a bowl wed to the spot where life had shut
them down like flotsam in the Wilshire tarpits
the stone age has a foot in the door always
double-ringed and home again I knelt beside
your grave the end of all our wandering
and after a squall of tears parted a tuft
of lawn sank the jet-and-silver shallow
in the soft earth nothing was in my head
I wasn't married more nor deeper merged
with you I couldn't be it was just a class
Cracker Jack prize a Havana cigar band
doubtless realer than sapphires yet the act
was *mindless* that's what I have to be to
breathe these days so I'm busily patting the grass
over the Zuni ring and maybe I start to soften
at least you had no agony at the end the ring's
all hidden and suddenly I'm moaning out loud
this very specific moan the echo of you
when I walked in the last day a horn sound
that knifes me still though I tore the walls down
for the drug to bring you back plus a needle
full of calm and once the drip was going talked
and talked by then you could only blink *yes*
but yes you heard me squeak us through the eye
of the needle one more time *It's okay Rog*
we'll turn it around you'll be here again by
morning and though I was wrong and lost you
like a diamond in the sea the final swell
as you rolled under was our old rowing

for one more tide vast as a blood moon stay
stay and voyage the far islands papayas
full of black pearls reefs of emerald Rog
the moaning wouldn't go away so the day of
the rings I mimicked you ventriloquizing
your last sound desolate as a sea-bell
trying to figure what the hurt was where
had we disappeared to then I froze mid-moan
saw it all in a blaze YOU WERE CALLING ME
my sailor brother oh I didn't know Death
had reached your lips muscles gone words dispersed
still you moaned my name so ancient wild and
lonely it took ten weeks to reach me now
I hear each melancholy wail a roar like
fallen lions holding on by your fingertips
till I arrived for how many drowning hours
to say *Goodbye I love you* all in my name
all by the howl that knows that after love
is nowhere who the fuck cares if we reassemble
as vermilion birds and fields of violets now
I hear how trapped how frantic was my friend
not to go it rings in the wind around me
like a signal sent by a dying star bursting
here in my dead heart a bloom of black light
calling WE ARE A MILLION MILES AWAY
SAY WE ARE NOT ALONE what all the rocks
are blazing with in the shivering blue of night
Do you see this stick sir a man asked Sidney
Smith *this stick has been around the world*
Indeed said Smith *and yet still only a stick*
what is there left to be spoken Rog just
that I'll be there momentarily a cry
in my ears like the lost horn in Brahms' First
as harborless I launch this lawless boat
veering like Ulysses for I cannot steer
and shriek your name together the deck awash

with jewels fine as sand nobody's ever been
anywhere they can't cover a thousand feet
of the road we walked two days before our trip
was off the rings have blown on the rockets
and all the riders to the outer limits are
scattered on the rain that bullets this gray sea
circle on circle so far gone no one's
seen a boat before the fish come out to gape
and somewhere men wake up and wonder *Wasn't*
there once a way out of here and back to sleep
you have to have been to Death to know the way
your moan will be the east wind of my going
the evening rose and lilac find me past
the Pole the pull of magnets moons mute dreams
I will console you yet though I have to belly-
crawl a cyclone orbiting out to the razor
curve of space if a man can call my name
at the whirlpool's edge then love is the last thing
no wonder I'm always packing till the moan
became my weather and compass my heart had
no place to go it followed the law and stayed
put but how did they think they could hold us
to one ground we met on a journey that is
why the world though stopped like a car wreck keeps
doubling back robbed of you as I am promising
shortcuts whispering of a Northwest Passage
I nearly lost my mind last week screaming
too late down an empty road but there you are
we're full of the same agony you for an hour
I for the rest the nameless dark hasn't
spared us a pang my love but give us this
if ever either of us lands we are one
cry one dream tight as a black gold ring

CURRENT STATUS 1/22/87

marginal no change T-4 four-sixty-five
as of 12/8 but the labs are notoriously
inexact nerdy white-coat sits eyeballing
his microscope counts the squiggles in a cubic
inch racks them up on his abacus and writes
his apt # on the lab slip thus I'm fifteen
less than August thirty-five more than June
this is not statistically meaningful nor am I
the walking wounded do not count the counting
begins at breakthrough how are my lymph nodes
how are they not a mere three-quarters
centimeter at the neck in the vampire spot
cm and a half in the armpit not suggestive
unless they harden or start to throb taking
four hundred milligrams *ribavirin* b.i.d.
the magic dose if results released 1/9
prove to be long-term of course when you cry
all day an afternoon can be frightfully
long-term but we mustn't muss the curve with
personal agendas equal dose *acyclovir*
ditto twice a day this part purest guesswork
doesn't attack HIV but seems to lower
the general viral bullshit level and besides
the cornflower-blue capsules go quite nicely
with the royal-and-white of the *ribavirin* rather
like the flag of an island nation which I am
bowels normal though I peer at each specimen
in the bowl like an oracle poking entrails
David E who just got back from the Rift
Valley where man began says if you flush
a toilet five feet south of the Equator
the spiral flows clockwise five feet north flows
counterclock this is the only non-medical
fact I have learned in two years moving now

to the head twenty milligrams *sinequan* for
despair no effect at all but may help
tip me over into sleep that little church
of the dark which bars me all its sacraments
add fifteen milligrams *dalmane* 2 A.M. for
the final knockout not the same as sleep
not even the same as night but a full-bore dose
of *sinequan* makes you Lennie in *Of Mice and Men*
within two weeks and you eat whole loaves of
Wonder Bread till your moon-face waddled body
humpty-dumpties off a wall no mouth sores
fevers sweats bruises like imploded orchids
nothing significant see you in March
to put it quite simply I'M DOING FINE
or as we say in California DOING GREAT
holding a shiv to the listener's throat as if
to dare contradiction the test-givers
bald numerologists and milligram chemists
all my tribe of shamans and not a one knows
the iron tests I watched you suffer the six
spinals three broncs your bone marrow sipped by
a ten-inch needle till you had enough numbers
to stump an algebra class pyramided like
a Mayan calendar exact to the second for
a thousand years by which time the last Mayans
stared out of stone eyes at the blue monkeys
who swarmed their decimal palaces my medicine
men can't see my condition is just a prefix
my vast pharmacopoeia no more than a grave
nod to you my friend who bore so many
milligrams we needed a gram balance like
a *charcuterie* in Paris tests of tests
my groping docs might just as well use leeches
for all they can touch my invisible disease
cracks on the heart don't blip on an EKG
thus no treatment sorry we don't cure life

Rog I am still in the anteroom of all
the useless measures leafing old *Peoples*
reading diplomas deep in my head I hear you
the night of the third intrusion your larynx
like slush from an extra milliliter's freeze
of *xylocaine* quelling your voice to a strangle
for two three hours *Why is this happening*
I don't know I said all the bells in my voice
untarnished and thought how no one had better
try to say why either or ever suppose
to know the worst take my pills like clockwork
because you took yours submit to the week's
bleeding because you fought like Theseus for
the white-crowned hill of your reason breakthrough
is the real thing when these are not just tests
of fate ball bearings in a wheel of luck they are
fate made visible which of my thirteen
pills would I give a dying child which one
ought the world to be taking morning and night
to feel this strange communion dose by dose
this set of printouts clinically healthy why
does that sound like a qualification is this
how being a hero starts or just dying
Ypres and Verdun men have lain down in certain
fields with all their unspent years but meanwhile
there is the fighting before that the target
practice I'm learning how to hold a sword
but there is no telling what I will do
when I get there stay at my side will you
so I don't do anything vain or cease to honor
you and all our brothers below the Equator

THE LOSING SIDE

Eve is five graves over or Brian is at least
d. 18 June two years old Eve elbow-rubs
the bronze plaque changes her flowers before
the least brown edge and sticks a pinwheel in
the ground above think what a brave toy it is
to flutter here on the hill catching the vague
random air like an amnesiac trying to
hum a few bars of the wind it's meant to scoop
and whir with a flip of Brian's backhand *You
have someone here* asks Eve the question half
withdrawn we none of us overstep on the hill
but of course we trade our terrible news neither
flinches we are the slaves of detail *He fought
so hard* I say the blizzard force of your
endurance reduced to fight-talk as if it
were equal combat man to man missing
the zen of war without armies attacked
on all sides drawing yourself like an arrow
so taut the tips of the bow pinched like tweezers
and all the *Iliad* stood in awe that's how hard
Eve nods *So did Brian* and there you have it
the sick nothing of life in its full dementia
the cloud of flies above Calcutta human
waves of boys choking the ditches of Basra all
still wailing as they run down Highway 1
out of Hue wings of napalm streaming not just
torture of the just like you but new improved
agony babies conscripted totally weaponless
not a comrade no word yet for enemy sent
to battle without a day in a sunny country
first no early world on a Kodachrome propped
in a foxhole Eve who's locked in the mother of
a two-year-old forever on Christmas Eve
having an extra pinwheel gave it to me

for you the grass being bare at our place
but for a pine cone minimal being my way
locked in a lost secret skittish of flowers
one look and the bloom's gone but the pinwheel
so improbable so detached from pain marked
your yard of the hill half the winter through
waves of rain then a week of clear Alaska
cold and sometimes I'd stare at the wind not
when it whipped itself to propeller speed
but tilting just a hair like a weathervane
ears cocked to a change in things or a stray breeze
turned it three times round like the light breathing
of Brian Crete is what I thought of then
the valley of the windmills cupped sky-high
on the mountain where Zeus was born d. 300
B.C. wasn't wild for the ride up holding out
for beaches but you won since on the road
there are always trade-offs caravans inching by
on hairpin trails swapping staples pirate
lore letters home anything not to go it
alone and here you are still winning Rog
I see it sudden as then mills by the hundred
wheeling each a perfect circle of sails
the valley agog with spinning the toys of Zeus
we're alive and well in Lassithi even now
playing the top of the world yet the sheer leap
is coy as a yo-yo memory lifts off easy
slapped out of string and canvas Kitty Hawk
Icarus red balloon pain is still the ground
where all flight crumples wingless Eve is right
the smallest thing will trigger it like plastique
and roar me back burning like phosphorus flesh
running like wax for her it's the smell of
laundry white from the dryer and cancel all
Wednesdays then comes the 18th of absolutely
anything and she homes to the hill where she

is cursed to love hereafter and hereafter
me it's Tuesdays Century City the canned
peaches at Hughes' there is nothing so nothing
it can't blow up in my face which is why I
stay in a locked house or wander out here
where pain's at least constant Eve and I swap
wars peacefully we've got nothing to lose
no more and she makes me see in her hard fight
not to think Brian could be walking now
that somehow we got to be men together
we got that far even if now I have to let
the wind blow through me whistling here and there
aching to find the boy who used to play me

MANIFESTO

unsolicited Adam S diagnosed 9/85
and lucky calls to say all sickness is self-
induced and as I start to growl oozes self-
beatification *taking a course in miracles*
he says and I bark my way out of his wee
kirk and savage his name from the Rolodex
another triumph of self-love like metaphysical
sit-ups a washboard ripple on the pre-
frontal lobe doubtless the work of Mrs. Hay
baghwan of the leper set Pooh-bear in hand
purveying love-is-you with an anchorlady's
do and Diane Arbus eyes straight-faced told
a reporter people in train wrecks bring it on
themselves *But what if somebody gets the virus
from a transfusion* WHAT ARE THEY DOING NEEDING
BLOOD IN THE FIRST PLACE pounces Lady Hay
every sucker in the ICU's to blame see
there are no microbes just self-loathing come
sit in a ring with St. Louise and deep-throat
your pale sore body lick your life like a dog's
balls and repeat after me I AM A MIRACLE
why do I care about all this who does it
harm shouldn't the scared and solo have a shot
at warding it off six months a year by dint
of mellowness well yes and no we need
the living alive to bucket Ronnie's House
with abattoirs of blood hand in hand lesions
across America need to trainwreck the whole
show till someone listens so no they may not
coo in mirrors disbarring the fevered the choked
and wasting as losers who have not learned
like Adam the yoga with which to kiss their own
asshole every tent revival mantra
is one less bomb tossed in the red-taped labs

of the FDA one less bureaucrat pelted
as he chews his Pilate's thumb toddling home
by limo to Silver Springs where all high-risk
behavior is curfewed after dusk forget it
the boys at Mrs. Hay's haven't an anarchist
bone in their spotted torsos miraculized
they may be but even if they last forever
will only love the one poor thing themself
and bury the rest of us spring in their stride
as they whistle home with the shovel thinking
I'm still here the level earth wide as they
can see strewn with burn and ruin like a
crash site but I admit it I love you better
than me Rog always have you're no different
all the migrainous interchange with crooks
and fools lines at the post that inch like Poland
dogged nerves of a day's wage how much self
is functional by Thursday afternoon unless
it has a weekend place remote as Na Pali
green as the light on Daisy's dock the boys
of Hay are learning how to laugh again
but what if one never forgot in the first
place oh boys I warn you now joy alone
will not protect you have it all you can
lie if you have to say you believe in
Oral Roberts's eighty-foot Jesus with
the ransom note but keep your miracles small
my friend and I we laughed for years on end
and the dark fell anyway and all our people
sicken and have no rage the Feds are lying
about the numbers the money goes for toilet
seats in bombers the State of the Union
is pious as Pius washing his hands of Hitler
Jews are not a Catholic charity when is
enough enough I had a self myself
once but he died when do we leave the mirror

and lie down in front of the tanks let them
put two million of us away see how quick
it looks like Belsen force out all their hate
the cool indifferent genocide that locks up
all the pills whatever it takes witness
the night and the waste for those who are not yet
touched for soon the thing will ravish their women
their jock sons lie in rows in the empty infield
the scream in the streets will rise to a siren din
and they will beg us to teach them how to
bear it we who are losing our reason

THE HOUSE ON KINGS ROAD

they will take me out feet first the orphan house
may not even notice right off for houses
are slow and set in their ways probably not
till the FOR SALE sign is stabbed by the front steps
will it groan in its sleep not till the movers
locust through bundling tagging the odd lot
of our mute remains will its Yale locks seize
like clotting blood desperate to keep us home
but as for now it's our last stand the halfway
house we thought to rest in going up except
the way is vertigo down the summit was just
a view of Fuji never meant to be scaled
only to gaze on far when houses fall
in Sophocles the blood of a king's name
is sown with salt downstage is hip-deep in
courtiers the princesses are led away
from ballet class to do their last lift for
a firing squad but what happens to people's
rooms the chair just so to catch the morning
the drawer of pennies the unmade bed aswirl
with the night's turning does anything manage to
memorize the place before it's trucked off
or is nobody's room permitted the smallest pause
unless a spinster's left to keep it in amber
a few years more but the auctioneer can wait
the quill on Dickens's desk is exactly where
he laid it everyone else is a slippery tenant
who can blame a house for being leery

always left in the lurch gas off phone cut
whatever time remains let the brief museum
of Kings Road be all mine I am the Board
of Trustees I am the Hoving I decide
what's out what's in vaults and I alone will
know the hours prepared to shutter like Paris
on the merest whim Starlite Tours idles
below at Chevy Chase's then up at the top
by Steve Martin apparently we are a highly
comic canyon our pedigree rich as Rue
de Fleurus Bacall and Bogie in living noir
champagning away the forties at 1600
Here's looking at you kid eight-forty-one
a month seemed an act of madness till it
stubbornly never went up like rent imagine
an IRS deduction for finding safe harbor
for the heart life's a roof my gentle housemate
lost at the front door still I bawl *I'm home Rog*
not that I really expect to meet you pouring
a glass of milk but the layout here is pregnant
as a stage mad to get in on the act *As You
Like It* poolside *Lear* in the back bedroom
and me the perfect audience all applause
fixed roof your diary scrawls *skimmed pool pasta
for supper* stuff you wouldn't suppose worth
the ink yet somehow it breaches the wall
within the wall more than memory more than
the pivot of event calls us home shoring
time with casual embraces unremarkable
as sky no set like Juliet's balcony
no histrionics star turns curtain calls
just the putting a house in order most
gay men live a bare half hour a day middle
of noplace airshaft rooms stacked with *Playbills*
socks balled tight as summer camp picking up
after themselves as if they keep a spare

mom in the closet up and down the city
the CEOs with the bearded ladies the pencil-
thin monsignors in Scarlett drag bachelors
live in bachelor flats can always be counted
to square a table need no china of their own
or knives inhabit their charm like tortoises
the landlady sweeps them clean in a day if they
chance to die but they die in a little hole
offstage so dinner is not delayed in small
towns they never leave home at all but sleep
in footed flannel pajamas merit badges
pinned in a row on the chest of drawers begging
the question wouldn't you think anywhere
would be a move up refrigerator crate
under 101 heating vent Eighth and Olive
up a fucking tree you have to crave your own
room before all else track it hammer it
steal it life may deal you a snowy doorway
leave you a gypsy lose your shoes and John
Doe tagged to your ankle but the dream house
is worth it it got you somewhere die in
its shady yard bougainvillea rippling
like a coral reef gold on the west windows
or only reach the lookout stare at the house
impossible on the far hill well at least
it's there it exists depart in peace your sigh
will merge with the mountain's echo beckoning
some just out of high school some in the army
one by one they set out in a terror of hope
visioning the place and the friend with a key
its threshold level with life as the cabin
on Walden world enough and nine tall trees
it's our house Rog I've got all the papers
so what if the legalese says *single man*
and *single man* beside our separate names
the law lies like the church lies the elders

cane their moonstruck sons and play at castles
Writing may be either the record of a deed
or a deed Thoreau says okay just this once may
this be a deed lawyerproof filed at the hall
of records that two men ceased to be single
here in a house free of liens and the rule
of sorry kings and sometimes would look up
from a book from peeling an apple their bright
astonished eyes would meet and nearly falter
gladness is like looking at the sun how can
Death untwine them or the room in the room
where they have one name oh my love tell me
where you are in the study writing Follain
laughing on the phone a bowl of pistachios
shucked beside you standing in the courtyard
shears in hand like a dousing rod surveying
the shape of an hour's pruning well then we both
must be taking a nap curled like spoons on
a rainy Sunday terror and evil banished
like the snakes in Ireland even fast asleep
you know you are holding the key and you must
keep it in trust for the children of children
who want you dead and maybe the timidest son
will know his name find his burning friend and come
unlock the dream a month before you went
you cried *What happened to our happy life*
staring blind out over the garden Rog
it's here it's here I know because I am
the ghost who haunts us I am the last window
sir tread lightly who bargain for this house
you are sporting with kings on a high road
despite the sifted gray of time where things
are atomized the white chairs under the elm
the wall of books laid brick by brick the lamp
pooling on the blue-bound Plato as we held
our ground through August let the material go

46

what you cannot buy or have in your name
is the ghost of a touch the glancing stroke
as a man passes through a room where his love
sits reading later much later the nodding head
of the one on the other's shoulder no title
usurps that place this is its home forever

III

LAST DAY AT MOLERA BEACH

> *I tell myself cold comfort that her aware-*
> *ness and beauty are dissolved into the*
> *world, and make it more beautiful. But an*
> *old superstition keeps me praying silently:*
> *"Make Una joyful, wherever she is."*
>
> —ROBINSON JEFFERS

the one path I can run in my head light-shod
a half mile from the coast road to the water
starred with sun you park where the Big Sur bends
and homes seaward its dry bed cobbled with
oyster-gray stones autumn lies beaten gold
on the hills no rain since April then you come
to the campers' meadow never more than ten
the wanderers back in school then a sudden grove
of eucalyptus where one flawless October
we saw the monarchs clinging in the leaves
by the millions the whole species wintering
in a swarm each black and tangerine fan
flexing its single facet as if Fabergé
had taken to the trees deer in the grove
and the hard shell of Molera's cabin its logs
brute as telephone poles don't ask me who
Molera was his land and his name deeded
to keep the river-mouth free for he's as gone
as anything man now leave the menthol cool
of the trees and cross through a chest-high field
you can hear the breakers roaring up ahead
like your own blood in a cupped shell the next
stand is laurel and alder so thick-knit
the path's a green tunnel careful you must
walk narrow for the underbrush foams here
with poison oak red-splashed whether to warn
or beckon it can't decide you come out

on the bank where a half bridge two feet wide
spans the low river right at water level
rude as a railroad tie flung down the single
man-cobbled compromise with the fatal
divide of things and the winter current will
submerge it but not now now you can walk
to the middle and suspend in the eagle
core of Big Sur pearly as the heart of
a chambered nautilus the autumn water
of the river-mouth still as a millpond look
inland the heaving curves of the coastal range
riding granite like a school of humpback whales
through here the river has left like a graduate
course in time this lavish savannah fit
for lions all this and the sea so wide is
the eye at the great folds of the world where
fresh and salt contrive the seed medium
of life but you can't stay go from the bridge
through a mirror thicket of bay laurel
hugging the left bank hunkered down as if
it knows it is the last thing of land and
fears the sea do not fear like the laurel
head over that rise of dune Molera Beach
sweeps south banked by headlands you're one end
of a kind of bay its 5-mile curve like the in-
step arch of a quarter moon stand still now
be where I was last September packed off
because I was falling apart and my friend
was on I.V. *pentamidine* stable and holding
the in-laws in from Chicago *go ahead*
Paul you can't go on like this relax relax
but never would've left Rog if you hadn't
promised to talk me through it never driven
north all night terrified of miles if I'd known
where you'd be in a month but let that go
I went and for three days hiked like a scout

the druidical bluffs and glens the hawk's roost
high on sunset each wind shift and long fog
warping the lone cypress crooked as bonsai
yet couldn't stop thinking when can I call
again or a nurse would say you were sleeping
and I'd bump in circles like a wing-shot gull
frantic under the redwoods by the phone booth
till finally I'd reach you and cry *I can't*
I can't be here without you how you'd sleek
my feathers ease me down coaxing postcards
sending me out like a falcon off your arm
for I was still our eyes to prey on every
lion slope and chalk ridge the final sighting
from Big Sur reported to you like a ship
deep at sea belling the weather about to come
I think I knew I was there to take leave
of the place the whole time wherever I'd stand
low tide at Pfeiffer Beach feet impressed like
fossils a crag like the prow of a wrecked
destroyer shoaled in the boiling surf a white
wave shooting the broken hull *take a good look*
I'd whisper barely there but holding because
I could tap my spring with the dial of an O
three times a day oh source of all that roams
open to the sky in me the wall of my heart
breached by a tidal surge the famished wave
given the years can bore right through granite
how many times have we been here Rog reckoning
tracing paths that change but do not alter
mute together gazing rapt at the slow
clock of seafall seasoned as a pair of otters
belly up in the kelp beds sunning the phone
locks down at UCLA at nine-thirty
all through the night call I'd be shivering
dancing the cloud of my white breath curling
up through the redwood spires to the diamond

dome of night as we traded the day's numbers
deer sightings blood counts X-rays cloudless
as the steeps of Ventana Cone till all in all
Big Sur and you were doing just terrific
let them not ever allow the slightest thing
more to be built in that numinous land
of parched gold keep it free of accretion
as Homer's Ithaca what Jeffers called it
but thank Hermes for ITT its buried vein
of voices coursing beneath the cataracts
so men can be two places together at once
or call it a third place where every last
syllable between us is a path running there
in the giants' garden sheer to the riddled
Pacific and here in our heads we managed
this farewell tour by pure technocracy
the same that kept us afloat two precious years
so don't finger me as a naturalist please
a fast car credit card and person-to-person
got me here not philosophy now reader
if you've held firm and still stand on the lip
of Molera Beach let me tell you about
goodbye if you walk south on the hard sand
between the tides where it gleams like polished
marble wrinkled like a snowdrift the bluffs
like an earth-shook wave of land heaved up frozen
at full crest a quarter mile past the nudists
past the wind-chill past even the girl on
the roan stallion at the foot of the bluff
where the March tide has undermined there are
hollows full of windblown sand fine as talcum
there I traced with a naked finger P & R
like a Beach Boys' song for no other reason
than to tell my friend at the night call it's not
there now even if it were March is bare
hours away are we getting the hang of it

every day is the last you will ever do
something learn to turn your back complete
as you walk the other way say *never again*
as to whether your soul will linger a million years
because you loved it well if you like
it's a nice superstition on my last day
I took a good look *so long* and turned bound
for a loss more calamitous than the end
of the sea off Point Sur Light I can run there
in my head any time Rog easy as I run
to you but you have become in the meantime
an ocean all your own so that is where
I beach now and swim in and out of the sea-
caves no time bound in iron tanks across
my shoulders night and day I ride the swell
and tumble headlong having no appointment
anywhere else the phone is dead of course
the moment on the beach would give its life
to stay but remember every man who ever
reached Molera thinks he discovered it new
stunned like Drake and how do you bring this home
to your king or in his case queen well you don't
it stays staying is how it grew so huge
but to leave it gladly slipping no stone
in a pocket on your final vacation no
souvenirs will see you home besides we still
had a month left in our own river-mouth lolling
in the sun-warmed water like fish about to
walk on land for the edges of change are steep
with love till the sea and the river are one

DREAMING OF YOU

What is anyone? What is he not?
Man is a dream of a shadow.

—PINDAR

one I never told you a month after
the verdict I came in the bathroom looked
around the shower door and you were dead
sitting back like Marat water to your waist
your head against the wall tilted as if
dozing torso muscles quick and beaded
like you just came in from swimming this
being the slow millisecond of the dream
you utterly you so still but all your beauty
holding its last breath then my lungs explode
and screaming I sweep you up in my arms
we reel out into the bedroom you are so
deadweight and nowhere I carry you will
ever bring you back I wake with the scream
in my blood it never never goes the dream
is a fear so deep from the next day on
my life has suffered an irreversible stroke
pulling me underwater circuits blown
and I am slurred all my extremities blue
like frostbite it may be years before I
know what a book is somehow I act my way
through the dead of the day the only other
option is to scream the night you went
wasn't half so loud as the dream though there
the scream I was swallowing shattered Baccarat
as far as Chicago and no next morning burned
it off like fog now my dreaming is flawed
by the sleep pills I don't start shooting till
I'm half awake but none of that Hitchcock stuff
with the bathtub once a mere three-line sketch

you in the hospital sleeping wake and say
Did you talk to those guys meaning the interns
who came to announce the meningitis thirty-
six hours before you died *yes* I answer
oh good reassured you close your eyes to sleep
through the worst of it if I wake in tears
and cry all morning it's joy at having
seen you you'd hardly been gone a week then
and the real scene that the dream cleared was all
panic and pounding terror you couldn't talk
those guys were jerks so you see it's the best
sort of imagining that clip of a dream
oh good I recall it better than anything
ever occurred in broad daylight give me night
give me more of it I wish to be an expert
on darkness and all it conjures wish to sleep-
walk with you no matter how queer a scene
the crooked synapses of my brain cast us in
a dream is never the one line long enough
what's even worse we can't go walking after
to watch from the canyon rim while the west
burns midnight they are brief they are shadows
they evaporate I wake I forget them
but if they're all I have then let them come
cascading just this week I dreamed we were
crying nothing else but that me sitting
on the bed beside you so much losing more
to be lost but I'll take sorrow to be
with you this all connects I promise Rog
having been dreaming of you since I was
fourteen oh a best friend brief vaporous
shadows then to find you in the flesh all
dreaming receded to the bottom of the night
silent hyperkinetic as a two-reel Chaplin
flickering like mica but now with you gone
my drowned imagining throbs to the surface

57

for air I'm a dreamer it's a wonder I put
my shoes on in the morning this latest one
Saturday night is me at the top of my form
we are walking in some kind of park brisk
and talking intently neither of us sick
I can't tell you how I relish being there
shoulders grazing as we quicken our way
you speak first but anyone can see we've been
talking forever *Sometimes Tom has to travel
by himself* Tom is the boy in my script with
time to burn nineteen but meaning also me
oh no I say *oh yes* you counter but not
truculent so sweet-tempered in fact it's
all talk nobody's trying to win the point
notice that *yes* and *no* like a flipped coin
the old chess of opposites attract besides
would you travel alone farther than I
if the coin were reversed or seek the dark
like me what's the opposite of insomnia
sleeping all day coma perhaps just death
or is it the love of dreams a willingness
to live in clips dispensable as curls
of footage on the cutting-room floor quick
close-up cut to the chase what did I miss
it's all middle over before you know it
freeze frame on us in the park end credits
and out now play it back every man is
his own screen fueled by a VCR echoing
like an old wound in the rain swiveling time
think of your wildest dream Rog isn't it
queer I rocked you out of a hundred horrors
over the sudden years and can't recall one
monster scare just the gathering you awake
the brief cling like a still *It's all a dream*
come come I will meet you beyond the moon
in the amphitheater my slumbering heart

it doesn't matter what riddles we speak how
circular the logic it's us we are not
making it up since day has got us nowhere
hold fast the bottomless night the snow beard
of Rip Van Winkle billowing like a down
comforter is that my Chaplin friend oh good
walk through the bedroom wall with me walk out
to where the Buddha dreams the world be a
fragment like an ode on marble erasing
in the rain sleep be our blue drink of life
wide as a camera turned on the morning sky

BROTHER OF
THE MOUNT OF OLIVES

Mine, O thou lord of life, send my roots rain.
—GERARD MANLEY HOPKINS

combing the attic for anything extra
missed or missing evidence of us I sift
your oldest letters on onionskin soft-
cover Gallimard novels from graduate school
brown at the edges like pound cake and turn up
an undeveloped film race it to SUNSET
PLAZA ONE-HOUR wait out the hour wacko
as a spy smuggling a chip that might decode
World War III then sit on the curb poring over
prints of Christmas '83 till I hit paydirt
three shots of the hermit abbey on the moors
southeast of Siena our final crisscross
of the Tuscan hills before the sack of Rome
unplanned it was just that we couldn't bear
to leave the region quite the Green Guide barely
gave it a nod *minor Renaissance pile*
but the real thing monks in Benedictine white
pressing olives and gliding about in hooded
silence Benedict having commanded *shh*
along with his gaunt motto *ora et labora*
pray work but our particular brother John
couldn't stop chattering not from the moment
he met us grinning at the cloister door
seventy years olive-cheeked bald and guileless
no matter we spoke no Italian he led us
gesturing left and right at peeling frescoes
porcelain Marys a limpid row of arches
across the court like a trill on a harpsichord
little did he know how up to our eyeballs
we were on the glories of Florence the Bach

geometry of the hill towns their heart-
stopping squares with the well in the middle
and a rampant lion on the governor's roof
we'd already scrutinized every *thing* and now
before we left wished to see it peopled
going about their business out of time
keeping bees holy offices raisin bread
as if nothing had happened since Galileo
instead this voluble little monk pulling us
into the abbey church its lofty Gothic vault
overlaid in sugared Baroque plaster like a bad
cake then Brother John grips us by the biceps
and sweeps us down the cypress-paneled choir
to the reading desk where the Gutenberg
is propped on feast-days he crouches and points
to the inlay on the base and there is a cat
tail curled seeming to sit in a window
every tiger stripe of him laid in jigsaw
as we laughed our rapturous guide went *mew mew*
like a five-year-old *How long have you been here*
we ask a question requiring all our hands
fifty years he tosses off as if time had
nothing to do with it one hand lingering
on my shoulder is it books we like then come
and we patter round the cloister in his wake
duck through a door up a stone stairs and peer
through a grill wrought like a curtain of ivy
into the library its great vellum folios
solid as tombstones nobody copying out
or illuminating today unless perhaps
all of that has died and there's a Xerox
glowing green in the abbot's study John
pokes you to look at the door carvings it seems
he is not a bookish man but who has time
to read any more we must descend and see
the frescoes fifty years without the world

pray work pray work and yet such drunken gaiety
gasping anew at the cloister's painted wall
clutching my hand before the bare-clad Jesus
bound at the pillar by the painter so-called
Sodoma the parted lips the love-glazed eyes
JUST WHAT KIND OF MEN ARE WE TALKING ABOUT
are we the heirs of them or they our secret
fathers and how many of our kind lie beneath
the cypress alley crowning the hill beyond
the bell tower how does one ask such things
with just one's hands then we took three pictures
me and John John and you you and me *click*
as the old monk takes my arm I'm certain now
that he likes touching us that we are a world
inside him whether he knows or not not that
I felt molested I can take care of myself
but a blind and ancient hunger not unspeakable
unsayable you think he knew about us Rog
how could he not pick up the intersect
the way we laughed the glint in our eyes as we
played our Italian for four hands but my sole
evidence is this sudden noon photograph
the two of us arm in arm in the cloister
delirious gold November light of Tuscany
washing our *cinquecento* faces splashing
the wall behind us a fresco of the monks
at dinner high above them in a pulpit
a reader trilling in Latin you can't even
eat without *ora et labora* and we look
squinting at John as if to wonder how
he will ever click the shutter right it's like
giving a watch to a savage but we look
quite wonderful you with the Green Guide me
clutching the pouch with the passports we look
unbelievably young our half smiles precisely
the same for that is the pierce of beauty

that first day of a rose barely started
and yet all there and Brother John so geeky
with the Canon A-1 did he even see what
he caught we look like choirboys or postulants
or a vagabond pair of scholars here to
pore over an undecoded text not religious
but brotherly enough it's a courtly age
where men are what they do and where they go
comrades all we look like no one else Rog
here's the proof in color now the tour is over
we are glided into a vestibule where cards
slides rosaries prayers that tick are gauntly
presided over by a monk senior to John
if not in years then officialdom the air
is strict in here we cut our laughter short
this one's got us pegged right off this keeper
of the canonical cash drawer withering John
with a look that can hardly wait to assign vast
and pointless rosaries of contrition we buy
the stark official guide to Monte Oliveto
leave a puddle of lire *per restauro*
for restorations and then we're free of His
Priestliness and John bundles us off still
merry and irrepressible too old perhaps
to fear the scorn and penitence of those
racked by sins of the flesh who never touch
a thing and ushers us out to the Fiat
bidding us safe journey who's never been
airborne or out to sea or where Shiva
dances or Pele the fire-god gargles
the bowels of the earth we wave him off
and leap in the car we're late for Rome flap
open the map but we're laughing too *Did that*
just happen or what and we drive away
winding up past the tower towards the grove
of graves where the tips of the cypress lean

in the breeze and a hooded monk is walking
head bent over his book of hours in passing
I see that it's John wave and grin *rividerci*
startled at his gauntness fixed on his text dark
his reverie no acknowledgement goodbye
that is the whole story you know about Rome
and flying tourist opening weeks of mail
putting a journey to bed and on and on
but I've thought of John ever since whenever
the smiling Pope makes another of his sub-
human attitudes the law he drives our people
from the temples and spits on the graves of his
brother priests who are coughing to death in cells
without unction and boots the Jesuit shrink
who calls all love holy he wants his fags
quiet *shh* and I try to think of John
and the picture he saved three years for me
till the lost roll of Tuscany came to light
and turned out to hold our wedding portrait
the innocent are so brief and the rigid world
doesn't marry its pagans any more but John
didn't care what nothing we professed he joined
us to join him a ritual not in the book
but his secret heart it doesn't get easier Rog
even now the night jasmine is pouring
its white delirium in the dark and I
will not have it if you can't I shut all
windows still it seeps in with the gaudy
oath of spring oh help be somewhere near
so I can endure this drunk intrusion
of promise where is the walled place where we
can walk untouched or must I be content
with a wedding I almost didn't witness
the evidence all but lost no oath no ring
but the truth sealed to hold against the hate
of the first straight Pope since the Syllabus of

64

Errors this Polack joke who fears his women
and men too full of laughter far brother
if you should pass beneath our cypresses
you who are a praying man your god can
go to hell but since you are so inclined
pray that my friend and I be still together
just like this at the Mount of Olives blessed
by the last of an ancient race who loved
youth and laughter and beautiful things so much
they couldn't stop singing and we were the song